The Nature Kid's Guide to
AARDVARKS

DAVID ANDERSON

LP Media Inc. Publishing
Text copyright © 2026 by LP Media Inc.
All rights reserved.

For information address LP Media Inc. Publishing,
30012 Variolite St NW, Princeton MN 55371
www.lpmedia.org

Publication Data

Aardvarks
The Nature Kid's Guide to Aardvarks — First edition.

Summary: "Learn all about Aardvarks, the Nature Kid Way"
— Provided by publisher.

ISBN: 979-8-89818-263-2

[1. Aardvarks – Non-Fiction] I. Title.

Title: The Nature Kid's Guide to Aardvarks

CONTENTS

Dusty Digs 4

African Homes 6

Pig Sized 8

Built Bizarre 10

Super Sniffers 12

Tough Skin 14

Ant Diet 16

Tongue Traps 18

Deadly Danger 20

Dig Deep 22

Waddle Walk 24

Night Shift 26

Lone Rangers 28

Finding Mates 30

Cute Cubs 32

Mom Knows 34

Ancient Adapters 36

Spot Them 38

DUSTY DIGS

DID YOU KNOW?
Old aardvark burrows become homes for warthogs, porcupines, and even hyenas!
4

Scritch! An aardvark digs into the warm, dusty earth.

Aardvarks live in warm, dry places. Open grasslands and light woods are their favorite spots. They need lots of space to roam.

At home, these animals live in **burrows**. A burrow is a tunnel dug under the ground. It keeps them cool when the African sun beats down.

Each aardvark may use many burrows. It moves from one to the next as it hunts. Some burrows have several rooms and tunnels stretching 40 feet long. A good burrow is like a cozy underground home!

AFRICAN HOMES

Thump! An aardvark pads across the wide African plain.

Aardvarks are found only in Africa. They live south of the big Sahara Desert. More than 20 countries have these funny animals.

You can find them in Kenya, Nigeria, and South Africa. No other place in the world has wild aardvarks. Africa is their one and only home.

Aardvarks roam through **savannas** and forests, traveling far and wide. If the soil is soft enough to dig, they may be close by. What a great land to call home!

PIG SIZED

The name 'aardvark' means 'earth pig' in Afrikaans, a South African language!

Thud! A big aardvark steps out, looking like a small pig.

An aardvark is bigger than most people expect. From the tip of its long snout to the end of its tail, it stretches about five feet — roughly as long as a bed.

A grown aardvark weighs around 130 pounds, about the same as an average Great Dane dog. That is a lot of animal packed into a strange-looking body.

And strange is the right word. Aardvarks look a little like pigs, a little like rabbits, and a little like nothing else on Earth. No other animal shares their shape.

BUILT BIZARRE
DID YOU KNOW?
Aardvarks have about 20 teeth, but none of them are in front—and they never stop growing!

Sniff! An aardvark pushes its long snout into a dirt mound.

Aardvarks have a very odd body. A long, tube-shaped snout sticks out from the front. Big, tall ears stand up on top of their head like rabbit ears.

Short, thick legs hold up a round body. Each foot has four strong claws made for digging. A heavy tail drags behind as they walk.

No other animal looks quite like an aardvark. Every strange part helps it stay alive. This odd shape is perfect for life in Africa.

SUPER SNIFFERS

Sniff, sniff! An aardvark crawls out of its burrow and sniffs the evening air.

Aardvarks have an amazing sense of smell. Their nose can detect ants and termites buried underground. They follow the **scent** right to the nest.

Those big ears help too. Aardvarks can hear tiny bugs moving under the dirt. Even the softest sounds are easy for them to pick up.

Aardvark eyes are small and weak. They do not see very well at all. But their powerful nose and ears more than make up for it.

TOUGH SKIN

Scratch! Claws scrape a termite hill looking for a meal!

Aardvarks have very thick, tough skin. It is like wearing a leather coat all the time. Biting bugs can barely get through it.

This tough hide helps when they dig into ant nests. Angry ants try to bite, but it does not hurt much. The aardvark just keeps on eating.

Even big animals have a hard time biting through an aardvark's skin. It acts like armor. This natural protection is one of their best survival tools.

Aardvark skin is so tough that sharp thorns and biting soldier ants cannot break through!

ANT DIET

DID YOU KNOW?
Aardvarks also eat a fruit called the aardvark cucumber — it grows underground and needs aardvarks to spread its seeds!

Crunch! An aardvark munches on a mouthful of termites.

Aardvarks love ants and termites. Those tiny bugs are their favorite meal. One hungry aardvark can gobble up 50,000 bugs in a single night!

All those bugs keep aardvarks healthy and strong. Without ants and termites, they would not survive. Bugs are their fuel.

Aardvarks do not chew their food at all. They swallow bugs whole. Their tough, muscular stomach grinds up the food for them.

TONGUE TRAPS

An aardvark's sticky tongue can stretch about 12 inches—as long as a ruler!

Slurp! An aardvark's sticky tongue zaps up a line of ants.

Aardvarks catch their food with a long, sticky tongue. It darts in and out super fast. Each lick scoops up a bunch of bugs.

First, an aardvark rips open a mound with its powerful claws. Then it pokes its long snout inside. Its tongue shoots out and grabs the bugs before they can escape.

The tongue is covered in thick, gooey spit. Bugs stick to it like glue. It is the perfect tool for catching a wiggly meal.

DEADLY
DANGER

Stalk! A leopard spots an aardvark out in the savanna at dusk.

Lions, leopards, and hyenas all hunt aardvarks. These big predators sneak up in the dark. An aardvark must always stay alert.

Large pythons are a danger too. They hide near burrow entrances and wait. When an aardvark comes out, the snake can strike fast.

Being out at night is risky business. Aardvarks use their sharp ears and nose to stay safe. One wrong step could mean big trouble.

Young aardvarks face even more dangers—eagles, wild dogs, and jackals all hunt them!

DIG DEEP

Whoosh! An aardvark dives into its burrow to escape the leopard.

When danger is close, an aardvark digs fast. It can vanish underground in just two minutes. Dirt flies everywhere!

Once inside, it blocks the tunnel with loose soil. This stops any hunter from following. The tunnel becomes a safe hiding spot.

Aardvarks can also run if they need to. They zigzag and dart from side to side. But digging fast is always their best escape trick.

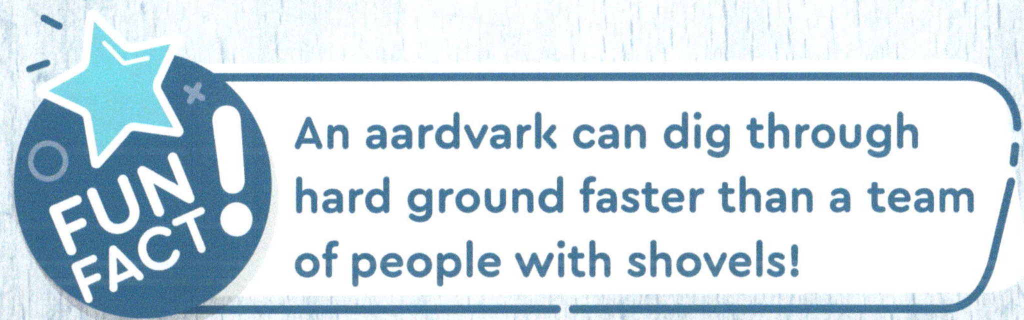

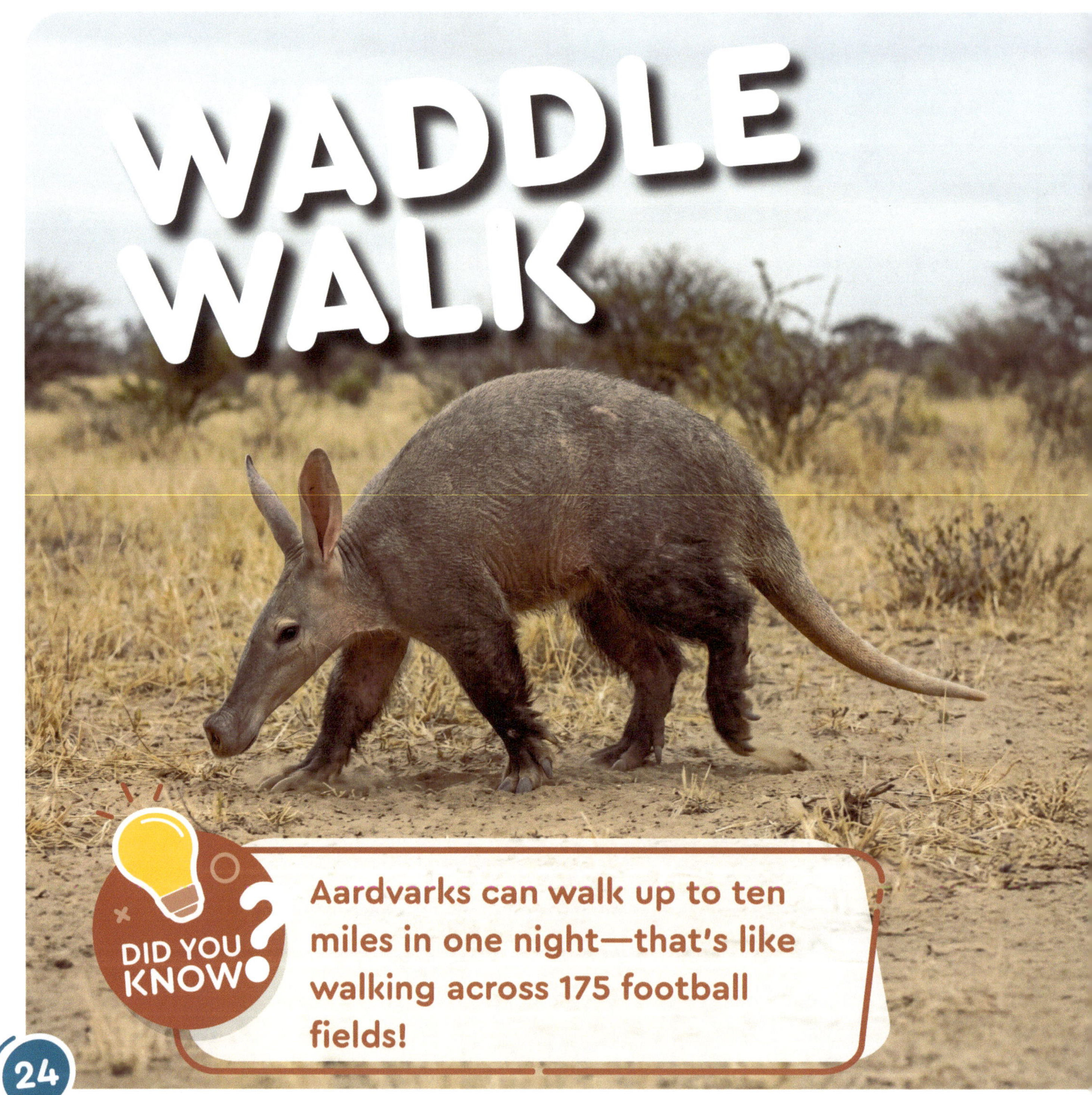

WADDLE
WALK
DID YOU KNOW?
Aardvarks can walk up to ten miles in one night—that's like walking across 175 football fields!
24

Plod! An aardvark shuffles along on its big, flat feet.

Aardvarks walk in a slow, funny way. They waddle side to side on short legs. It looks like they are in no hurry at all.

As they walk, they weave back and forth. This zigzag path helps them sniff more ground. They check for ant nests along the way.

Sometimes an aardvark stops to dig a quick test hole. It pokes its nose in, smells around, then moves on. They walk and sniff all night long, covering miles of ground.

NIGHT SHIFT

Yawn! An aardvark wakes up as the sun starts to set.

Aardvarks are **nocturnal**. That means they sleep all day and come out when it gets dark. This schedule keeps them safe from many hunters.

At sunset, an aardvark peeks out of its burrow. It sniffs the air and listens carefully. If all seems safe, it heads out to eat.

All night long, it walks and hunts for food. At dawn, it hurries back to its burrow. Then it curls up and sleeps until the next sunset.

In cool weather, aardvarks sometimes sunbathe outside their burrows to warm up!

LONE RANGERS

Shhh! A lone aardvark creeps through the grass all by itself.

Aardvarks like to be alone. They do not live in groups or herds. Each aardvark has its own space to roam and hunt.

An aardvark claims a big area all its own— sometimes several square miles. It walks through this space each night, rarely bumping into another aardvark.

Mothers and babies are the only pairs you will see. After about six months, the young aardvark goes off on its own. Life alone is the aardvark way.

FINDING MATES

A mother aardvark carries her baby inside her for about seven months—almost as long as a human pregnancy!

Snort! A male aardvark follows a scent trail in the dark.

A male aardvark lifts his nose and sniffs the air. He is looking for a female. He may walk for miles to find her.

The two aardvarks spend only a short time together. After they meet, the male goes away. The female is on her own again.

Soon, a baby will be growing inside her. She keeps eating and digging to stay strong. She has a big job ahead!

CUTE CUBS

DID YOU KNOW?
A newborn aardvark weighs about four pounds—but it will grow to be 30 times heavier!

Squirm! A young aardvark snuggles and sleeps in its cozy burrow.

Aardvark babies are called **cubs**. Most of the time, a mother has just one cub. The tiny baby is born inside a safe, warm burrow.

A newborn cub is pink with wrinkly, hairless skin. Its eyes stay closed at first. After about two weeks, the baby finally opens its eyes to see the world.

The cub grows fast. After just a few weeks, it follows mom outside for the first time. The world out there is big, dark, and full of new smells!

MOM
KNOWS

Nuzzle! A mother aardvark gently sniffs her tiny baby.

Mother aardvarks take care of their cubs all alone. Dad does not help at all. Mom feeds her baby milk for the first few months.

She also teaches her cub to dig and find food. At first, the baby just watches and learns. Bit by bit, it tries digging on its own.

By six months old, the cub is ready to leave. It goes off to find its own place to live. Mom has done her job well.

A young aardvark starts eating insects when it is about three months old—but still drinks mom's milk too!

ANCIENT ADAPTERS

Scrape! An aardvark digs for bugs, just as its family has for ages.

Aardvarks are ancient animals. Scientists have found fossils showing that creatures very much like today's aardvarks have roamed Africa for a very long time. Their bodies have barely changed at all.

Digging and sniffing for bugs has kept them alive through it all. These skills still work just fine. Aardvarks know exactly what to do. Aardvarks also help the land around them.

Their digging mixes up the soil and helps plants grow. They play a big part in keeping the African wilderness healthy.

SPOT THEM

The San Diego Zoo has one of the most well known aardvark exhibits in North America — and has helped breed aardvarks in captivity!

Wow! An aardvark eats some treats from a dish at a zoo.

Most kids will never walk through the African savanna at night. But that does not mean you cannot meet a real aardvark up close.

Many zoos across North America keep aardvarks, and they are worth seeking out. These animals are most active around feeding time, when their long tongues and powerful claws really get to work.

Check your nearest zoo's website before you visit to see if they have aardvarks on exhibit. Some zoos offer keeper talks where you can get even closer and learn more.

GLOSSARY

burrow

A hole or tunnel dug underground by an animal

cub

A baby aardvark

nocturnal

Active at night and sleeping during the day

savanna

A wide, flat grassland with few trees, found in warm parts of Africa

scent

A smell left behind by an animal to send messages to others